The Marine Corps in Action

Nathan Aaseng
AR B.L.: 10.5
Points: 3.0

UG

THE MARINE CORPS in ACTION

THE MARINE CORPS in ACTION

Nathan Aaseng

Enslow Publishers, Inc.

40 Industrial Road   PO Box 38
Box 398   Aldershot
Berkeley Heights, NJ 07922   Hants GU12 6BP
USA   UK

http://www.enslow.com

Library of Congress Cataloging-in-Publication Data

Aaseng, Nathan.
    The Marine Corps in action / Nathan Aaseng.
        p. cm. — (U.S. military branches and careers)
    Includes bibliographical references.
    ISBN 0-7660-1637-4 (hardcover)
    1. United States. Marine Corps—Juvenile literature. [1. United
States. Marine Corps. 2. United States. Marine Corps—Vocational
guidance. 3. Vocational guidance.]   I. Title. II. Series.
VE23 .A927 2001
359.9'6'0973—dc21

                                        2001000181

Printed in the United States of America

10 9 8 7 6 5 4

To Our Readers: We have done our best to make sure all Internet addresses in
this book were active and appropriate when we went to press. However, the
author and publisher have no control over and assume no liability for the material
on those Internet sites or on any other Web sites they may link to. Any comments
or suggestions can be sent by e-mail to comments@enslow.com or to the address
on the back cover.

Illustration Credits: All photos are courtesy U.S. Department of
Defense, except for the following: United States Marine Corps, pp. 6,
69, 75; National Archives, pp. 15, 18, 21, 22–23, 28–29, 31, 38, 40, 42,
48–49, 96–97, 101, 110; George Bush Presidential Library, p. 36;
National Aeronautics and Space Administration, p. 76.

Cover Illustration: United States Marine Corps (background); U.S.
Department of Defense (inset).

Contents

The Marine Corps' 24th Expeditionary Unit, aboard the U.S.S. *Kearsarge*, was the American military force closest to downed Air Force pilot Scott O'Grady.

The Mission and Role of Today's Marines

Air Force pilot Scott O'Grady flew his F-16 over northern Bosnia, helping to enforce a no-fly zone ordered by the United Nations over that strife-torn region of southeastern Europe. Suddenly, a deadly surface-to-air missile burst through the clouds beneath him. Serb forces, the main targets of the no-fly policy, had fired the sophisticated missile.

Before O'Grady could take evasive action, the missile slammed into his plane and cut it in half. The pilot managed to eject, but the American military had no idea if he was alive. For six days, there was no word on O'Grady's fate. Then, in the early morning hours of June 8, 1995, an American search plane made faint radio contact with the downed pilot. Somehow he had survived and avoided capture in the densely wooded hills twenty miles behind Serb lines.

Send in the Marines

As soon as Admiral Leighton Smith, commander of the North Atlantic Treaty Organization (NATO) forces in Southern Europe, got news of O'Grady's situation, he put in a call to the Marines. The Marines' 24th Expeditionary Unit, located in the Adriatic Sea aboard the U.S.S. *Kearsarge*, was the American military force closest to the scene. At 3:00 A.M., the unit's commander, Colonel Martin Berndt, took Smith's call. Smith asked how soon the Marines could go in and rescue O'Grady.

"One hour's notice," came the reply.[1] The commanders considered their options and the risks. Without food and water except for what he could scrounge off the land, O'Grady was weakening. Fast action was needed. The decision was made to go in at dawn, even though daylight would make the rescue team an easy target for Serb surface-to-air missiles. They would have to go in quickly and get out fast before the Serb forces closed in.

At 5:05 A.M., two CH-53 Sea Stallions lifted off the deck of the *Kearsarge*. The helicopters carried a rescue team of forty-one Marines, including riflemen, scouts, medics, communications experts, reconnaissance experts, and an interpreter. For forty-five anxious minutes, the helicopters circled the ship, waiting for jet fighters that would provide support to arrive. At last, defended by forty warplanes, the rescue team headed inland. Two Sea Cobra helicopter gunships led the way, flying just above the dense fog banks that shielded their presence from the Serbs.

At 6:35 A.M., the gunships spotted a yellow flare that O'Grady had lit to mark a landing area. Nine minutes later, the first of the Stallions landed. Out rushed twenty Marines to establish a perimeter of defense. The second helicopter arrived and had barely touched ground when O'Grady burst out of the woods and ran to it. The Marines hoisted him aboard and took off. Both aircraft had been on the ground no more than three minutes.

As the Stallions flew away, their covering aircraft detected Serb radar locking on to the rescue team. They requested permission from their superiors to destroy the site. Fearing that the action would escalate what had been a small-scale conflict, the commanders denied permission. The helicopters would have to escape on their own.

The Serbs launched several surface-to-air missiles that sailed close but did not hit the mark. Flying at 175 miles per hour, the pilots dipped down to within 100 feet of the ground to avoid further missiles. Although rifle bullets struck the Stallions, no one inside was hurt. By 7:30 A.M., O'Grady and the rescue team were safely on board the *Kearsarge*.

America's 911 Force

The flawless rescue of Scott O'Grady was just one of many dangerous jobs performed by the United States Marine Corps in the 225 years of its existence. Those jobs have changed over the years to keep pace with the military's changing needs. As the smallest of the military services, the Marine Corps has always had to struggle for its part of the action. Traditionally the least funded of the services, the Marines have had to make do with less equipment and technology than other forces. This has forced the Marines to be able to readily adapt to the demands of changing times.

Originally, Marines were intended to serve as soldiers aboard Navy ships. Eventually, however, their role has evolved into that of a multipurpose, highly mobile, small-scale fighting force.

"Light enough to get there and heavy enough to win," is one of the Marine Corps' slogans.[2] This means that since Marines are not bogged down by heavy armor and their numbers are small, they can deploy, or move, quickly to wherever they are needed. Yet once they arrive, they pack enough firepower to accomplish any short-term military objective. These objectives can range from small rescue actions such as the O'Grady mission to major military action. For example, when Iraq seized Kuwait in 1990 and threatened to overrun Saudi Arabia and other Middle Eastern nations, it was the Marines who spearheaded the first line of defense. More than 45,000 Marines, equipped with 100 tanks transported from supply bases in the Indian and Pacific Oceans, were able to establish a formidable defensive front near Kuwait until the slow task of assembling the larger and more heavily armed Army forces could be accomplished. The Marines are equally comfortable protecting U.S. citizens in trouble spots around the world and in carrying out humanitarian tasks such as the peacekeeping missions in Haiti and Somalia during the 1990s.

The Few, The Proud

Like the other military services, the Marine Corps offers a wide variety of careers and training opportunities. Even a small operation, such as the O'Grady rescue, involved communications experts, weapons and guidance system experts, and aviation specialists as well as combat

Two CH-53 Sea Stallions, like the one pictured here, flew behind Serbian lines to rescue pilot Scott O'Grady in the early morning hours.

troops. Also, mechanics, food service, transportation, public affairs, and construction personnel provided essential support for this rescue.

Marines consider themselves a special group of warriors who demand the best from themselves and from each other. They take enormous pride in being an elite fighting force. Only those who pass their rigid standards for discipline, strength, toughness, spirit, pride, teamwork, and professionalism earn the right to be called Marines.

Marines form a special bond with all Marines past and present who have served under the Corps' eagle, globe, and anchor emblem. The Marine Corps motto, *Semper Fidelis*, means "always faithful." The Marines believe that a Marine has a duty to uphold the honor of the Corps at all times. No matter what their occupation, they carry with them a sense of belonging—of being one of "the few, the proud, the Marines."[3]

History of the United States Marine Corps

The idea of creating a group of soldiers to travel by sea and fight on land dates back thousands of years to the Phoenicians. These raiders sailed great distances and landed just long enough to storm towns along seacoasts and plunder the wealth that they found. The Vikings of Northern Europe used similar tactics during the Middle Ages.

Throughout the centuries, however, most countries divided their military forces into two separate groups: the soldiers, who fought for control of the land, and the sailors, who fought for control of the seas. During the seventeenth century, France and the Netherlands found that this division left a gap in their military forces. Both began training some of their sailors in the techniques of infantry combat.

Following the lead of France and the Netherlands, King Charles II of Great Britain authorized a regiment known as the Royal Marines under the command of the Navy in 1664. Whenever Great Britain was involved in a war over the next century, it recruited Marines to aid its cause. One of those times occurred in 1739, when the British recruited four regiments of Colonial Marines from their American colonies for a South American military action. George Washington's half brother Lawrence was among those recruits. At the outbreak of the American Revolution in 1776, the British military forces included nearly 4,500 Marines.

Birth of the U.S. Marine Corps

The British held such an overwhelming sea power advantage that the colonists could not challenge them head-on. Raids made by volunteer sailors and fishermen offered the only American opposition to British naval power at first. Some of these sailors sought riches by picking off British merchant ships and carrying away their cargoes. A group of Massachusetts mariners then formed a seaborne militia known as the Marblehead Regiment. The regiment performed more typical Marine duties such as harassing enemy ships during Britain's siege of Boston in 1775.

Later that year, some American military leaders proposed an expedition to destroy the British military base at Halifax, Nova Scotia. The only practical way to attack the base was from the sea. Such an action was tailor-made for Marines. So on November 10, 1775,

This is believed to be the first flag of the United States Marine Corps and the Continental Navy. The coiled snake was painted on the drums of the early Marines.

the Continental Congress called for the formation of "two battalions of Marines to serve for and during the present war between Great Britain and the colonies."[1] The plan called for the Marines to be drawn from George Washington's regular army. Washington, however, could not spare anyone from his command. As a result, the two battalions were never formed, and the Halifax raid was never launched.

Captain Samuel Nicholas
(1744–1790)

The first United States Marine Corps officer was Samuel Nicholas of Philadelphia. Most likely a tavern keeper in civilian life, Nicholas received a commission as captain on November 28, 1775. After serving in the naval raid on the Bahamas, Nicholas returned to Philadelphia to recruit more Marines. In November 1776, he and four companies of Marines were pressed into emergency service to aid General Washington's battered army. Captain Nicholas's Marines fought through Washington's New Jersey campaigns during the winter of 1776 before the companies disbanded.

The Americans did attempt to put together a small navy to protect the coast and rivers from raids and to harass British shipping. Small groups of Marines were recruited, and by early in 1776, the Americans had 234 Marines stationed on five sailing ships. For unknown reasons, the tiny fleet left the American coast and sailed to the Bahamas. There the Marines saw their first action, capturing two forts and forty cannons against very little opposition.

The United States Marines' tradition of adaptability arose in these early days. Some Marines fought as infantrymen in Washington's successful land campaign in New Jersey. Others took part in John Paul Jones's daring adventures on the seas. On April 22, 1778, Jones took the fight to the British shores by launching a raid on Whitehaven, an English port on the Irish Sea. At midnight, thirty Marines in rowboats caught the fort guard by surprise and set fire to a ship.

The next year, Jones's ship, the *Bonhomme Richard*, came under attack from the British warship *Serapis*. The Americans took a horrendous pounding until the Marines strapped the ships together, boarded the *Serapis,* and forced its crew to surrender.

Aside from a few isolated triumphs, though, the Marines were not a significant factor in the war. The Marine Corps commands were scattered through eleven of the thirteen colonies, and the number of Marines never totaled more than two thousand. By 1780, due to death or capture, only seven of the seventeen detachments of Marines remained active, and they had not gained much of a reputation as a fighting group. American general Benedict Arnold dismissed them as "the refuse of every regiment."[2]

Leathernecks

Once the Americans won their independence, they all but disbanded their entire military. Many believed that the constant turmoil of war that ensnarled the European nations was due to their tradition of maintaining huge standing armies. They hoped to avoid war by making the military a low priority and staying neutral in international disputes.

This idealism was put to the test, however, in the late 1790s. Encouraged by the British, pirates from the Barbary States of the North African coast (Algiers, Tunis, Morocco, and Tripoli) raided and plundered all shipping in the Mediterranean, sparing only vessels of Great Britain and its allies. Unable to defend its

Marines jumped aboard the British ship *Serapis* after it attacked the American ship *Bonhomme Richard*. In hand-to-hand combat, the Marines forced the British crew to surrender.

merchant ships in that area, the United States signed a humiliating treaty in which it agreed to pay $1 million to the Barbary States in exchange for protection for its ships. The countries of France and Great Britain then made matters worse by refusing to honor American neutrality in their wars against each other. Both seized American merchant ships carrying goods to their enemy.

Unable to defend its citizens and their property, the United States began to rebuild its dormant Navy. Included in this rebuilding was the revival of the Marines. In 1798, Congress passed an act establishing a Marine Corps of 848 men and 33 officers under the authority of the U.S. Navy. Marines were assigned to all Navy ships and given four main duties:

1. To serve as military police aboard ships.

2. To attack coastal towns and forts.

3. To maintain and defend U.S. coastal forts.

4. To board and capture enemy warships.

The Marines were given their own distinct uniforms, including the blue trousers with the red stripe still used as part of dress uniforms today. The Marines also endured the discomfort of thick leather collars designed to protect their necks against cutlass slashes. Although these unpopular collars were eventually abandoned, they earned the Marines the nickname "Leathernecks."

Lieutenant Presley O'Bannon (1776–1850)

Beginning in 1784, the United States paid the Barbary States not to attack U.S. ships in the Mediterranean Sea. However, in 1801, Congress refused to continue the payments. As a result, the pasha (ruler) of Tripoli declared war on the United States.

A free-spirited Virginian in search of adventure, Lieutenant O'Bannon led seven Marines and about 100 mercenaries on a five-week, 600-mile march across the desert from Egypt to Derna, a stronghold of Tripoli, in 1805. O'Bannon skillfully coordinated their surprise attack on the city with cannon fire from three U.S. ships offshore. Although two Marines died in the attack, O'Bannon's troops forced the surrender of the city. Tradition holds that the sword worn by Marine officers is a copy of the sword presented to O'Bannon after the victory.

From Tripoli to Montezuma

Disputes between the Navy and the Marine Corps over responsibility for certain duties nearly eliminated the Marines before they were even established. In 1803, however, an American squadron that was sent to blockade the port of Tripoli struck a reef. When the ships went down, 308 sailors, including 48 Marines, were captured by Tripoli and held hostage for ransom. In response, a group of Marines led a makeshift army in a 600-mile march and surprise attack on Tripoli's port of Derna. Although they forced the surrender of Derna, the victory accomplished nothing, because word arrived a day later that the United States had already succeeded in negotiating the release of the

The Marines raise Old Glory to fly for the first time over a foreign city, Derna in Tripoli.

hostages. Nonetheless, the Marines' daring and successful effort earned them public acclaim.

The Marines had to be content with this small victory while a permanent role was being found for them. The Marines accomplished little in the War of

1812. In fact, they saw no significant action other than defending Fort McHenry on the night that inspired Francis Scott Key to compose "The Star-Spangled Banner" and fighting in General Andrew Jackson's army in the victory at New Orleans.

As president, Jackson sent the Marines to Florida in the 1830s to dislodge the Seminole Indians who were refusing to yield to the United States' treaty demands. Although the Marines persisted for six years, they never fully accomplished their mission.

A decade later, when the United States declared war on Mexico, the Marines had to lobby hard to win a spot in the invading force under General Winfield Scott. At the last minute, a Marine

A battalion of Marines marching into Mexico City. The Marines helped capture, and later guard, the National Palace during the American occupation of the city.

regiment was hastily recruited and trained and then dispatched to join Scott's army. The Marines, under Lieutenant Colonel Samuel Watson, saw no part in any of the campaign's early battles.

In September 1847, Marines participated in the storming of the fort of Chapultec Castle, which guarded the entrance to Mexico City. In fierce hand-to-hand fighting, the American forces eventually took the castle, and soon thereafter, the capital city. Because of their guard duty experience, the Marines were assigned to guard the National Palace, once the home of the Aztec king Montezuma, during the American occupation of the city.

At about that time, an unnamed Marine penned some lyrics to a tune from a popular operetta. His effort began, "From the Halls of Montezuma to the shores of Tripoli. . . ."[3] Actually, the Marines had a greater role in defeating Mexican forces along the coast of California than in the capture of Mexico City. The song, which was eventually adopted as the official Marine Corps song, helped the Marines build their elite image.

Marines and the Monroe Doctrine

A political statement issued decades earlier brought the Marines a unique role in the country's foreign policy. In 1823, the U.S. government had announced its opposition to the European nations' efforts to establish and control colonies in the New World. Henceforth, the United States would take military action against any such attempts to interfere with the affairs of nations in the Western Hemisphere, a policy that became known as the Monroe Doctrine.

Over the years, the United States began to use this doctrine as an excuse for furthering its own economic interests south of the border. The highly mobile Marines became the government's primary tool for advancing its policies. For example, in the 1850s, the Marines were sent to Nicaragua to protect a ferry line owned by wealthy American railroad giant Cornelius Vanderbilt. When American business interests were threatened in Haiti, Panama, Argentina, and even China in the 1850s, the Marines sailed to the rescue. The native people were often resentful of this interference in their affairs, which created an atmosphere of distrust of Americans that has lingered for many decades.

The Civil War

The Marine Corps had almost no function in the nation's most costly military conflict, the Civil War. Its most noteworthy contribution came before the war actually started, when Colonel Robert E. Lee led a detachment of Marines that captured John Brown, who was trying to inspire an uprising to free the slaves at Harper's Ferry, Virginia.

Many Marine officers were southerners who joined the Confederate armies. However, the U.S. Marine Corps itself fought on the Union side, although its numbers were tiny and its achievements few. A group of 350 Marines, holding the middle of the Union line at the First Battle of Bull Run, broke and fled in panic along with the rest of the Union Army. A disastrous raid on Fort Fisher, North Carolina, wiped out 300 of the 400 Marines in the 3,500-man assault.

One result of the war was the change in the Marines' emphasis. Noting that increased firepower had made hand-to-hand fighting on ships obsolete, the Marines began to focus more on methods of traveling by sea to launch coastal attacks. This method of sea and land fighting became known as amphibious warfare.

The Big Stick

Following the Civil War, the Marines again appeared to be an outfit looking for a purpose. Exhausted by the war, the American public had no interest in military ventures. From 1865 to 1876, membership in the Marines was very sparse, dropping as low as two thousand. The only important U.S. military encounters during that time were the Indian wars in the West, in which the Marines were given no role. The Marines were reduced to policing a national railroad strike in 1877.

As the United States' influence in the world grew, it began to intervene more often in international crises. In the latter half of the nineteenth century, Marines traveled to Japan, Hawaii, Panama, South America, and the Caribbean to enforce U.S. policy.

In 1898, the United States went to war with Spain over U.S. interests in Cuba. Spain was no match for this growing world power and gave in within four months. The Marines distinguished themselves during this brief action by mounting a daring amphibious landing on the beaches of Guantanamo Bay in Cuba and by taking the Spanish-controlled Manila Bay in the Philippine Islands. Twenty-eight Marines were among the 250 Americans who died in the war.

The Marines' most dramatic action in defense of U.S. international policy to that date came in China in 1900. Fed up with having Western nations interfere in their affairs, a group of Chinese commonly known as the Boxers tried to drive out all foreigners. It was the U.S. Marines who led the defense of the international community in Peking against a ferocious onslaught.

When Theodore Roosevelt assumed the presidency in 1901, he had no qualms about sending in the Marines. "Speak softly and carry a big stick" was his policy, and the Marines were the big stick that he used to get results. The United States assigned the Marines to stop rioting in Haiti and battle rebel guerrillas in Nicaragua. When Colombia balked at allowing the Panama Canal to be built through its territory, Roosevelt sent the Marines to back Panamanian rebels who were more favorable to the canal. With all these demands, the Marine Corps was allowed to increase its numbers to over 7,500 enlisted men and 278 officers in 1903.

During the Battle of Manila, the Marines distinguished themselves by taking the Spanish-controlled Manila Bay in the Philippine Islands.

Captain John Myers

In 1900, during the Boxer Rebellion in China, Captain Meyers and his fifty-six Marines marched 120 miles from the coast, where they were serving guard duty on two ships, into Peking. There they rescued a number of foreign civilians, including Americans, trapped by Boxer rebels. The Marines held the main wall of a barricade against overwhelming numbers and increasingly desperate assaults for fifty-five days. Seven Marines died and ten were wounded protecting more than three thousand civilians from attack.

Devil Dogs

The Marines' performance during World War I did much to boost their reputation as an elite fighting unit. When the United States entered the war in 1917, the War Department was content to let the Marines sit on the sidelines. The massed armies slugging it out in trench warfare in the middle of Europe did not present the type of conflict the lightly armed, highly mobile, ship-transported Marines were designed to fight. However, the Marines lobbied hard to become part of the action. A brigade of nearly 8,500 Marines were assigned to defend a large section of woods known as the Bois de Belleau about 40 miles northeast of Paris.

Sensing that the arrival of the Americans would eventually tip the balance of the war against them, the Germans made a desperate attempt to break through the French lines, capture Paris, and force the French to surrender. After capturing the town of Château-Thierry in May 1918, the Germans advanced into some

IF YOU WANT
TO
FIGHT!

JOIN THE MARINES

Howard Chandler Christy, 1915.

A United States Marine Corps recruiting poster from World War I.

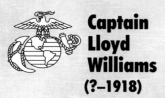

Captain Lloyd Williams

(?–1918)

Perhaps no one has demonstrated the Marines' fighting spirit more clearly than Captain Lloyd Williams. During World War I, Williams was in command of the Marines who reinforced the battered French Army at the Bois de Belleau in France, a forested area near the Marne River. After a fierce engagement with the Germans, the French commander ordered a retreat to a safer position. Williams's response was, "Retreat, hell! We just got here."[4] Ignoring the order, the Marines not only held their position but also drove the Germans out of the woods. Captain Williams was killed in battle a few days later.

woods, where they ran head-on into the Marines. The French commanders ordered the Marines to dig in behind their trenches and hold the line. The Marines, however, were not trained to sit still. They mounted a mobile defense so effective that the Germans asked for reinforcements to help them overcome these American *Teufelhunds* (devil dogs). Despite suffering more than a thousand casualties in a single day, the Marines refused to back down. Not only did they stop the Germans from advancing; they also drove them out of the woods in two weeks of intense fighting.

The failure of this German assault marked the beginning of the end for Germany. The French commander was so grateful for the Marines' effort that he ordered the woods renamed *Bois de la Brigade des Marines*, meaning "wood of the Marine brigade."

World War II

Ironically, the Marines' stellar performance at Bois de Belleau caused military experts to question whether there was any need for them. In France, they operated as an Army unit. In reality, the Army, with its heavy guns, tanks, and massed infantry, was more suited to such fighting. Many believed that improved firepower made the amphibious (land and sea) attacks for which the Marines were trained impossible.

The Marines, on the other hand, believed the time was soon coming when amphibious attacks would be crucial. Observing the growing power of Japan in the Far East and in the Pacific Ocean, they looked for ways to improve amphibious techniques. They organized amphibious training exercises in Cuba and Puerto Rico and began to redesign all their equipment and transportation.

After the Japanese attack on Pearl Harbor on December 7, 1941, the United States went to war with Japan. Desperate to stop the Japanese advance, the United States rushed the Marine Corps' First Division to the Pacific in late June 1942. With only five weeks of training and using untested equipment, the Marines stormed the island of Guadalcanal. The landing was the first American offensive of World War II. It was a success, although the Marines' lack of experience in such landings resulted in supplies' piling up on the beaches rather than going directly where they were needed. The Marines moved quickly inland, capturing a key airfield. But when the Navy aircraft carriers and other vessels left the area to fight elsewhere, they left the Marines vulnerable. The Japanese landed reinforcements and launched furious counterattacks. For six months the Marines fought in the dense jungle, stifling heat, and torrential rain. Although they suffered 3,000 casualties and 8,500 cases of malaria, they drove out the enemy and stopped the Japanese advance across the South Pacific.

The Marines eventually assigned six full divisions to combat in the Pacific, sweeping the Japanese from one island after another in a series of amphibious assaults. Some of these battles were extremely costly. At the tiny island of Tarawa, the landing craft got stuck on coral reefs, exposing the Marines to withering fire. More than 1,100 Marines died and 2,290 were wounded taking Tarawa.

Learning from their mistakes, the Marines achieved remarkable coordination in a series of increasingly difficult amphibious assaults. In July of 1944, they attacked the Japanese stronghold

Major General John A. Lejeune (1867–1942)

Lejeune took over as commandant of the Marine Corps in 1920, at a time when many experts thought that World War I had proved the Marines were obsolete. Lejeune crafted a new role for the Corps as "the first to set foot on hostile soil in order to seize, fortify, and hold a base"[5] from which the Army could carry out a campaign. Lejeune recognized the threat that Japan posed in the Pacific and established training in amphibious warfare to counter it.

of Saipan in the Mariana Islands to secure airfields from which the U.S. military could bomb Japan. The Marine victory cost 13,000 casualties. When the U.S. bombers had trouble making it back to Saipan after their missions, the military ordered the Marines to capture the Japanese island of Iwo Jima, which was only 670 miles from Tokyo.

The Japanese were determined to defend Iwo Jima at all costs. More than 23,000 defenders dug a remarkable network of tunnels across the island and waited for the attack. The 60,000 Marines who landed on the beach found themselves caught in what became the most savage and costly battle in the history of the Marine Corps. One participant wrote, "The deaths at Iwo Jima were extremely violent. There seemed to be no clean wounds; just fragments of corpses. It reminded one battalion medical officer of a Bellevue Hospital dissection room. Often the only way to distinguish between Japanese and Marine dead was by their legs [because the Marines wore canvas leggings and the Japanese had khaki trousers]. Otherwise identification was completely impossible."[6]

The Marines lost 5,900 men at Iwo Jima, with 17,372 more wounded.[7] Yet they won the undying admiration of the American people, symbolized by one of the most celebrated photographs in the world. Associated Press photographer Joe Rosenthal caught the spirit of the Marine Corps when he snapped a shot of six men planting a United States flag at the top of Mount Suribachi on Iwo Jima. The six worked as a

President George Bush speaks in front of the Marine Corps War Memorial in Arlington, Virginia. This statue depicts the raising of the flag on Iwo Jima by the United States Marines during World War II.

team, their faces all hidden or obscured, toiling for the honor of their country.

The Marines executed a total of 26 amphibious assaults in the Pacific during the war. In every case, they succeeded, although the cost was dear. Of the 485,000 Marines who fought during World War II, 20,000 died and 67,000 more were wounded.

Korean War

In June 1950, the United States and other members of the United Nations joined South Korea in fighting the Communist forces of North Korea, which were backed by China. The Korean War caught the U.S. military off guard. The makeshift forces, including the Marines who were sent to stem the North Korean attack, were pushed back into a small corner of South Korea, where they barely survived until reinforcements arrived.

U.S. commander General Douglas MacArthur called on the Marines to carry out a bold amphibious attack behind the North Korean lines at the port city of Inchon. The attack was extremely risky because the unusual tides at Inchon were suitable for a landing for only three hours in the morning and three in the afternoon, with no margin for error. But the Marines established a solid beachhead in their first landing and the reinforcements arrived like clockwork in the afternoon. The Marines quickly captured Inchon and the South Korean capital of Seoul. They continued to drive the North Koreans back up the coast while the U.S. Army pushed inland.

Marines lead a patrol on Wolmi Island, the gateway to the Korean city of Inchon.

The U.S. commanders pushed too far, however. As the Americans approached the Chinese border near the Yalu River in North Korea, a huge Chinese army suddenly came to the rescue of the North Koreans. A large part of the First Marine Division was surrounded at the Chosin Reservoir. Outnumbered five to one and short on ammunition, the Marines nevertheless fought their way out of the trap. Marching in subzero temperatures through rugged mountain terrain while fighting off ferocious attacks, the Marines made it back to safety. Despite nearly impossible circumstances, they brought out all of their dead and wounded as well as most of their equipment.

The rest of the war was basically a stalemate that finally ended with a truce in July 1953. More than four thousand Marines died in three years of fighting on the Korean peninsula.

Vietnam Nightmare

President Dwight Eisenhower used the Marine Corps as an all-purpose foreign crisis team during the 1950s. He sent Marines to evacuate American citizens caught in unrest in the Suez, Lebanon, and Venezuela. Eisenhower also assigned them to participate in humanitarian efforts in countries such as Morocco, Turkey, Greece, and Mexico that were devastated by earthquakes and floods.

Eisenhower's foreign policy decision that had the greatest impact on the Marine Corps was his support of the South Vietnamese government in the civil war

Brigadier General Lewis Puller
(1898–1971)

Born in Virginia, the aggressive Puller enjoyed a long and distinguished career as a combat leader. Known as "Chesty"—either for his thrust-out chest when he stood at attention or for his chest full of medals—Puller was the most decorated Marine in history. He earned his reputation battling Sandanista guerrillas in Nicaragua in 1929. He then solidified it by leading a hard-fought, hand-to-hand victory on the beaches and in the jungle and caves of the Pelelieu atoll in World War II. In Korea, Puller's leadership of one of the two major landings in the amphibious assault at Inchon and courage under fire during the near-disaster at Chosin Reservoir made him a national hero. (Below, a bugler plays "Taps" for the members of the First Marine Division who fell at Chosin Reservoir.)

between North and South Vietnam. (A former French colony, in 1954 Vietnam was divided into Communist North Vietnam and non-Communist South Vietnam.) Gradually, the United States became more and more involved in the Vietnamese conflict. Early in the 1960s, American advisors and weapons were sent to bolster the forces of the South Vietnamese government. In 1965, as North Vietnam increased its support of the Vietcong (South Vietnamese who opposed their government and fought with the North), the United States sent in combat troops.

The Marines were the first to arrive, in March 1965. As the conflict escalated, the Marines were placed under U.S. Army command and assigned to a sector in the northern part of South Vietnam. They chafed under orders that were foreign to their training and tradition: They were ordered to maintain a defensive posture, and most of their action consisted of conducting sweeps to clear areas of enemy soldiers, who would slip away into the countryside and return to conduct hit-and-run attacks as soon as the Marines left. In an effort to gain a decisive victory, the military kept increasing its troop strength. By 1967, 85,000 Marines were stationed in Vietnam. The most dramatic battles took place in late January 1968. First, a powerful North Vietnamese force attacked the Marine base at Khe Sanh. They succeeded in cutting off all roads to the base, leaving the Marines in a precarious position. A little more than a week later, the Vietcong launched the massive Tet offensive, in which they attacked

The first U.S. Marines land at Da Nang in South Vietnam in March 1965.

virtually every city and military base in the country. The Marines were pushed out of the ancient city of Hue in fierce fighting.

The Marines at Khe Sanh were saved by relentless air strikes, and they recaptured Hue after a grim one-month battle. But the heavy losses, including 205 Marines dead at Khe Sanh and 142 killed at Hue, discouraged the American public, which had been led to believe the war was going well. The United States began a strategy of withdrawing troops and turning the fighting over to the South Vietnamese Army, a process called "Vietnamization." The last Marine forces left the country on June 25, 1971, discouraged and disillusioned by the way the U.S. government had conducted the war.

More Marines served in the small country of Vietnam than fought in all of World War II. Marine casualties included 13,000 killed.

Corporal Robert O'Malley (1943–)

Corporal O'Malley was one of four brothers from New York City who enlisted in the Marine Corps. In the combat at An Cu'ong 2 during the Vietnam War, O'Malley single-handedly attacked a group of Vietcong in a rice paddy. He helped to evacuate wounded soldiers and had the remainder of his unit regroup to fight off an attack. Although seriously wounded three times, he refused evacuation until he covered his squad's boarding of a helicopter. For his valor, O'Malley received the Congressional Medal of Honor, an award he shares with roughly three hundred Marines in U.S. history.

Tough Times for the Corps

During the 1970s, morale in the Marine Corps slipped considerably. The long, costly, unpopular, stationary war for which the Marines were not suited had left many disillusioned. In addition, the enormous manpower requirements of the war in Vietnam had forced the Marines to accept lower standards in their recruiting. As a result, according to Brigadier General Bernard Trainor in 1978, "Many ill-adjusted, antisocial young men ended up in our ranks."[8]

One of the consequences of the disillusionment that occurred was the erosion of the tight discipline necessary to run an effective U.S. military. Journalist Arthur Hadley wrote, "From the end of the Vietnam War until 1978, U.S. soldiers were murdering their officers and destroying their equipment, drugs were rampant, weapons and facilities were neglected and poorly maintained."[9]

Furthermore, U.S. prestige abroad fell. Symbolic of the nation's military confusion was the takeover of the U.S. embassy in Tehran by Iranian radicals on November 4, 1979. A few Marine guards slowed the onrushing mob while others shredded secret documents. U.S. government officials ordered the Marines to surrender rather than face such overwhelming odds. Sixty-five U.S. civilians and thirteen Marines were held captive, and the United States was unable to obtain their release for over a year.

Four years later, the 24th Amphibious Unit was stationed in Lebanon as part of an international peacekeeping force. A yellow Mercedes truck, driven by terrorist suicide bombers and carrying several hundred pounds of explosives, crashed through the guard gate at the Marines' temporary barracks. The charge detonated, unleashing a tremendous explosion that destroyed the four-story barracks, killing 220 Marines and 21 other military personnel. This horrific event—involving the largest single-day loss of Marines since World War II—triggered inquiries into the state of U.S. military readiness.

Commandant Al Gray

A New Jersey native, Gray dropped out of college to join the Marine Corps in 1950. He fought in Korea, received a commission as an officer and served with distinction in the Vietnam War. Gray's performance as a Marine was so impressive that, despite his lack of education, he was named commandant of the Corps in 1988. It was Gray who revived the

Marine Corps' fighting spirit after its Vietnam decline, with his insistence that "Everybody has to be a warrior if they're going to be a Marine."[10]

Rebuilding the Marines

In the 1980s, the Marine Corps recovered, particularly after the appointment of General Al Gray as commandant. The Marines made a major effort to tighten their recruiting standards and instituted what Gray referred to as "warrior training" among their recruits.[11] Efficiency and pride shot up in the Marine Corps.

The Marine First Division carried out a vital combat mission during the early days of Desert Storm in the Gulf War. Pushing first into the country of Kuwait on the east and routing the Iraqis from Kuwait City, these troops wiped out thirty-four Iraqi tanks in close action. In addition, the Corps' professionalism and spirit in peacekeeping missions to places such as Somalia and Haiti has reestablished its reputation as an elite, flexible, highly disciplined, mobile fighting force.

Recruitment and Training

Since the end of the draft (compulsory military service) in 1973, the United States military has relied entirely on volunteers. The armed forces fill their ranks by recruiting young men and women from 17 to 28 years of age. Recruiters stationed at posts throughout the nation carry out Marine recruiting. They actively seek out young men and women who they feel would make outstanding Marines and encourage them to enlist.

Marine Recruiting Standards

Being the smallest of the military services, the Marine Corps can afford to be choosier in who it accepts. No one can be a Marine unless they have completed high school. In addition, the Marine Corps relies heavily on the Armed Services Vocational Aptitude

These young men are being sworn in at a U.S. Marine Corps recruiting station in New York City during World War I. Today, the Corps still relies on recruiting posts to help men and women volunteer for duty.

Battery (ASVAB) to determine a potential recruit's qualifications. This is a series of tests sponsored by the U.S. Department of Defense and administered without charge to any high school student interested in an armed services career. It consists of ten different tests measuring skill and interest in a variety of academic areas (such as verbal and math) and occupational areas (such as mechanical and electronic). The ASVAB not only gauges a person's qualifications for military service careers, but also helps match the person with a career to which he or she is best suited. The Marines offer an Enlistment Options Program, which guarantees even before they enlist that recruits will be assigned to the field in which their interests lie.

The Marines also have some basic physical requirements. Male recruits must be between 66 and 78 inches tall; female recruits must be between 58 and 72 inches tall. Those who are judged to be overweight may need to undergo a physical training program before they are accepted into basic training. Eyesight must be at least 20/200, correctable to 20/20. Those interested in aviation must have at least 20/30 vision, correctable to 20/20.

All applicants to the Marine Corps are screened for criminal backgrounds. Minor problems with the law are not an automatic disqualification, but prospective recruits who are not honest in providing information about their history may be rejected.

The term of enlistment may vary. Recruits generally enlist for four, five, or six years. Those who receive special training from the Marines are obligated to serve additional years. Ground officers must serve for a minimum of three and a half years after gaining their commission. Pilots of helicopters or turboprop aircraft must serve in the Marines for at least six years, while jet pilots must serve a minimum of eight years.

Marine Culture

All enlisted Marines report to military processing centers in their home regions for physical exams; they are then transported to one of two basic training camps. Those living east of the Mississippi River report to Parris Island, an isolated outpost on the Atlantic coast near Beaufort, South Carolina. The Parris Island facility, built in the nineteenth century, was originally a military jail. It was converted to a Marine recruit training depot in 1915, but it retains the no-frills look of its origins. Over twenty thousand Marines go through training at Parris Island annually, with roughly four thousand recruits in training at any one time. Marine recruits living west of the Mississippi train at a similar facility in San Diego, which has been in use since 1916.

All enlisted Marines undergo thirteen weeks of intensive basic training, which is three weeks longer than boot camp for any of the other military services. The Marines require the extra time primarily because their program places a heavy emphasis on teaching recruits about Marine culture—the Corps history and traditions and what makes the Marines different from other services. Throughout its history, the Marine

Corps has frequently been in danger of being disbanded or absorbed into one of the larger military services. Accordingly, Marines work very hard at distinguishing themselves from other military personnel, providing a unique identity. As one military expert observed, "Culture . . . is all the Marines have. It is what holds them together."[1]

The Marines spend time building community and teaching core values such as courage, honor, commitment, self-respect, respect for others, and loyalty. They strive to build the Marines into a close-knit family where everyone works together toward their objectives. Marine recruits are not allowed to use the word "I." Instead, they must refer to themselves as "this recruit." This instills the principle that Marines sacrifice personal wants for the good of the group.

Every Marine is expected to uphold the Corps' motto, *Semper Fidelis*, at all times. All recruits are steeped in Corps history so that they understand both the sacrifices that have been made and the reputations that have been won by those who went before them. They are constantly challenged to meet the high standards set by previous generations of Marines.

Drill Instructors

Upon arriving at basic training camp, the recruits are issued equipment and formed into platoons. The platoon serves as their family for the next thirteen weeks as recruits try to follow the leadership of a team of three drill sergeants who will control every waking moment of their lives. These drill instructors are intense, loud, and demanding as they whip a confused, scared platoon of recruits into a disciplined squad.

There was a time when Marine basic training had a reputation for being a physical and emotional nightmare, and drill instructors were stereotyped as abusive, almost sadistic, in their attempts to instill discipline. The worst example took place on April 8, 1956. Staff Sergeant Matthew McKeon, who was displeased with his platoon's progress, marched his recruits into Ribbon Creek, a tidal stream, late at night. They walked into a drop-off, and six recruits drowned in the mud and treacherous tide. Two more training deaths in the 1970s led military authorities to reexamine the Marine Corps' training methods. They found that the process of abuse had become institutionalized.[2]

At that time, the Marines revised their training program. Although the sergeants today are tough and demanding, they are not allowed to physically abuse a recruit. Drill instructors generally avoid the strong language for which they were once famous and instruct the recruits to report any incident of abuse to their superiors.

Warrior Training

The Marines are totally unapologetic about the fact that they train recruits to fight wars. According to a Marine Corps recruiting poster, "No one likes to fight, but somebody has to know how."[3] For the Marines, every member of the Corps is a warrior who must

In basic training, recruits are expected to give all of their energy when they do an exercise. This recruit gets directions from her drill instructor as she goes over the side of a rappelling tower.

know how to shoot a rifle. This philosophy dates back nearly two centuries to Marine commandant Colonel Charles Hayward. Hayward believed the U.S. Navy's success in the War of 1812 was due to its exceptional emphasis on gunnery practice, and so he decided to make every Marine a rifleman. A considerable portion of recruit training involves learning to care for and shoot a rifle.

Marine recruits also learn to march in precise formation. They work on improving physical fitness and developing confidence with long runs, calisthenics, basic hand-to-hand fighting, and obstacle courses that include rope climbing and jumps from great height. They also spend time in the classroom learning Marine Corps history and philosophy and memorizing the structure of the Corps.

No recruit is allowed to consider himself or herself a Marine until they have earned the title by fulfilling the demands of basic training. Not all recruits are able to handle the lifestyle or the physical, mental, and emotional demands of being a Marine. One out of every seven recruits who arrives at Parris Island or San Diego "washes out"—either quits or is dismissed from the Marines before the end of training. This is about double the washout rate in the Army.

With their focus on pride and tradition, the Marines place a huge emphasis on graduation from basic training. Many Marines consider the formal graduation ceremony one of the highlights of their life. It signifies that they have passed the test and earned the respect that all Marines give to other Marines. That respect lasts for a lifetime. Once a person becomes a Marine, he or she is considered part of that select group for life. According to a former Corps member, "There are no 'ex-Marines.' We always identify ourselves as former Marines."[4]

Following graduation from basic training, recruits take part in four weeks of instruction in advanced field and combat skills, either at Camp Lejeune in North Carolina or at Camp Pendleton in California. Most Marine recruits then enter a job skills training program. There they receive training in one of over three hundred Marine Corps occupation specialties in thirty-six career fields. Job skills training can last from four weeks to a year, depending upon the complexity of the skill. Marines who have served well for a number of years may qualify for a special-duty position such as drill instructor or embassy guard. These responsibilities require further training. Prospective drill instructors attend a special school that prepares them to mold raw Marine recruits into confident, polished units. Embassy guards can assume their duties only after passing a tough six-week course at the Marine Security Guard School.

Education in the Marines

Education is important to the Marine Corps. More than 95 percent of enlisted Marines attend a formal school following combat training. The Marine Corps College Fund makes up to $50,000 available for

After getting through basic training, this Marine accepts congratulations at the graduation ceremony. For many Marines, this is one of the proudest days of their lives.

college to qualified Marines who enlist for a minimum of four years. All Marines on active duty receive up to 75 percent tuition assistance. Even those stationed overseas and in conflict zones can get advanced education. The Corps sent civilian instructors to work with Marines stationed in Bosnia during the 1990s and often provides instructors aboard ships for individuals who want to take classes while stationed at sea.

Marine Corps Officers

The Marine Corps requires that all of its officer candidates have a four-year college degree. It does not have its own equivalent of the Army, Navy, and Air Force service academies for training officers. A large part of its officer training is done in conjunction with the Navy. Those wishing to become Marine Corps officers may follow that career path by entering the U.S. Naval Academy at Annapolis, Maryland. Following a four-year program, Naval Academy graduates earn a bachelor of science degree. Some graduates receive commissions in the Marine Corps, while a greater number go on to careers in the Navy.

Prospective Marine Corps officers can also enroll in a Naval Reserve Officers Training Corps (NROTC) program; such programs are in place at more than sixty colleges and universities nationwide. Participants carry a typical college course load with an emphasis on naval science.

Exceptionally qualified enlisted Marines who are college graduates can also move into the officer ranks

Shown is General Carl E. Mundy, commandant of the Marine Corps from 1991 to 1995. The commandant is the highest position in the Corps.

even though they have not attended the U.S. Naval Academy or an NROTC program. These candidates undergo a rigorous screening and evaluation program before they are accepted into the Platoon Leaders Class or the Officers Candidate Class. The chances for a Marine recruit to advance into officer ranks are far greater than for recruits in the other military services. For example, in the late 1990s, 26 percent of new Marine officers came from the enlisted ranks as compared to 9 percent of new Army officers.

Regardless of how they enter the officer ranks of the Corps, Marines must serve four years of active duty once they attain their beginning officer status as second lieutenant. Upon receiving their commission, all Marine Corps officers attend the twenty-six-week Officers Training School at Quantico, Virginia. The Quantico facility was constructed in 1917 on land purchased from the Quantico shipbuilding company. Aviation officers follow this with a program of flight instruction that lasts from eighteen to twenty-four months. Ground officers attend specialty officer schools for a somewhat shorter period of time.

Because of its emphasis on discipline, teamwork, and the individual's being less important than the team, the Corps does not cut its older, higher ranking officers any slack when it comes to physical health. Twice each year, all Marines under the age of forty-six must pass a strenuous physical fitness test to remain a member in good standing.

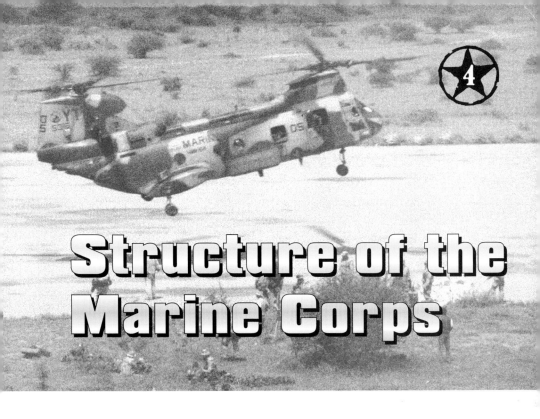

Structure of the Marine Corps

The Marine Corps is much smaller than the other military services, and its basic purpose has changed considerably over the years. From time to time, many of its duties have overlapped with those of specially trained units in the other services. For these reasons, the size and the structure of the Marine Corps have been topics of considerable debate over the years.

The Place of the Marine Corps in the Military

Because of their early role as soldiers stationed aboard ships, the Marines have historically been put under the overall supervision of the Navy. As the Marines evolved into a mobile, quick-strike land force, many observers felt that their duties and function had more

★ 63 ★

in common with the Army than with the Navy. Accordingly, in the early twentieth century, President Theodore Roosevelt decided to fold the Marine Corps into the U.S. Army. The Marine Corps' supporters in Congress, however, thwarted the president's plan by refusing to authorize money for the Navy until Roosevelt revoked the order.

The addition and growing role of aircraft to the military arsenal in the 1930s and 40s created a new problem in defining and assigning the responsibilities of the military services. During World War II, the Army and Navy each developed their own aircraft to assist their military objectives. Following the war, there was considerable debate over whether one military branch should control all the aircraft, whether they should be split, whether a new branch should be created, and where the Marine Corps fit into the overall picture.

Modern Reorganization

Congress solved the dispute by passing the National Security Act of 1947 that entirely reorganized the

In Haiti, Marine Corps sniper Corporal Joseph Cooper, of the 2nd Marine Battalion, 2nd Marine Regiment, 2nd Marine Division Sniper Platoon, provides reconnaissance and security.

American military structure. It revamped the president's cabinet, eliminating the Department of War and creating a new Department of Defense to oversee the entire scope of the nation's military needs.

The 1947 National Security Act also reorganized the U.S. military into three major components: the Army, the Navy, and the Air Force. The Act placed the Marine Corps in its traditional place as an independent operation under the overall supervision of the Secretary of the Navy. The 1947 Act set the Corps' level at three divisions totaling 200,000 troops. Since that time, the size of the Marine Corps has been subject to change, depending on the nation's military needs. Under President William Clinton at the turn of the twenty-first century, Marine Corps strength was maintained at 174,000.[1] The Marine Corps' share of the nation's military budget is presently around 6 percent.

The Marine Corps' status as something more than just an offshoot of the Navy was strengthened in 1973 when, for the first time in its history, the Marines were granted a representative on the Joint Chiefs of Staff. The Joint Chiefs of Staff is the president's select group of military advisors.

Marine Corps Structure

The structure of the Marine Corps is based on the number three. The largest Marine unit is the division, and there are three of them. Each division is made up of three infantry regiments (along with artillery and support units). Each regiment is made up of three battalions. There are three companies to each battalion, three platoons per company, three squads per platoon, and three fire teams for each squad. Marine infantry units in descending order from the largest to the smallest are division, regiment, battalion, company, squad, and fire team.

The infantry units work together with artillery, armor, aircraft, and support units. A Marine battalion operating in the Bosnian-Serb combat zone in the late 1990s consisted of 18,000 Marines, supported by 17 tanks, 74 armored vehicles, 33 artillery pieces, 12 attack helicopters, and 74 attack airplanes.

Civilian Control

The military is asked to operate in life-and-death situations where it is crucial that decisions be made immediately and carried out without question. For this reason, the Marine Corps, like all military organizations, has a tightly organized chain of command. In any situation, the highest ranking person bears responsibility for making the decisions, and all others are expected to follow them.

The supreme commander of all U.S. military forces is the president. The secretary of defense, who is appointed by the president and approved by the Senate, is next in line and is responsible for the overall operation of the Department of Defense. Within the Department of Defense, the secretary of the Army, secretary of the Navy, and secretary of the Air Force

Former Secretary of Defense William Perry talks with a group of Marines during a tour of the peacekeeping mission in Haiti. The Marines are guarding the perimeter of the port facility during Operation Uphold Democracy.

supervise their respective branches. The Marine Corps is among the responsibilities of the secretary of the Navy.

Although the president, secretary of defense, and secretaries of the Army, Navy, and Air Force may have vast military experience, they do not serve as members of the armed forces, but rather as civilians responsible for the operations of the military. The reason for this is the United States' long and unwavering tradition of democracy that prohibits the military from making policy decisions. All military personnel in the United States are thoroughly schooled in the principle that only government officials elected by the people, and administrators appointed by those officials according to law, have the right to make policy. The military exists only to carry out the policies decided upon by the democratically elected government. This principle has provided tremendous stability to the United States government. While military takeovers are the most common method of transferring government power in much of the world, the U. S. military has never made any attempt to take control of the government. In this country, every transfer of power from one party to another has taken place peacefully in the form of elections.

Leadership Within the Marines

Within the Marine Corps the highest position of authority is that of the commandant, who is appointed by the secretary of the Navy. The commandant is chosen from among the Marine Corps officer ranks, but the position does not necessarily go to the officer with the most seniority. In fact, one of the most highly respected Marine Corps commandants in recent years was Al Gray, who came up through the ranks before a college degree was a requirement for a Marine officer. Today he would not even be considered eligible to be an officer in the Marine Corps.

Despite being more closely connected with the Navy than with the Army, the Marine chain of command is like that of the Army. The highest Marine Corps rank is general, followed in order by lieutenant general, major general, brigadier general, colonel, major, captain, first lieutenant, and second lieutenant.

The Marine Corps command structure is less top-heavy than that of the other military services. There are roughly 18,000 officers compared to 155,500 enlisted Marines. This ratio of one officer per 8.6 enlistees is nearly half that of the Air Force. This is a result of the Marine Corps' heavy emphasis on recruiting and training, creating a Corps in which everyone is a reliable rifleman, and its recognition of group rather than individual achievements. Nearly half of all Marines serve in the lowest three ranks, a figure that is twice that in the other services.

The Enlisted Ranks

Everyone who enlists in the Marine Corps, except for those in the officer

Marines are eligible for challenging assignments when they reach the rank of corporal. These two corporals take position in a partly completed fighting hole during a war games exercise.

programs, enters as a private. However, they are called recruits until they graduate from basic training. Privates who have served six months of active duty move up to the rank of private first class. The next step is lance corporal, followed by corporal.

Marines are not given responsibility for supervising lower ranked Marines until they reach the rank of corporal. At this level, they are also eligible for more challenging assignments, such as embassy duty, sea duty, barracks duty, and recruiting. Corporals can advance to the rank of sergeant—the highest rank that noncommissioned Marines can achieve. Sergeants are considered the backbone of the Marine Corps because they have direct training and supervisory responsibility for the privates, who are by far the most numerous members of the Corps. The high regard in which the Marine Corps holds its sergeants is evidenced by the fact that since 1850, sergeants have been as entitled as commissioned officers to the honor of wearing a sword in ceremonial dress.

There are several levels of sergeant, beginning with sergeant and staff sergeant. A Marine enlistee who advances to the level of gunnery sergeant is considered a senior-level leader and may be involved in administrative duties. Beyond gunnery sergeants are the ranks of master sergeant, first sergeant, master gunnery sergeant, and sergeant major. Following is a list of Marine Corps ranks for commissioned officers and enlistees, from highest to lowest.

Marine Corps Ranks, from Highest to Lowest[2]			
Officers		**Enlisted Personnel**	
Pay Grade	**Rank**	Pay Grade	**Rank**
O-10	General	E-9	Sergeant Major of the Marine Corps
O-9	Lieutenant General		Sergeant Major
O-8	Major General		Master Gunnery Sergeant
O-7	Brigadier General	E-8	First Sergeant
O-6	Colonel		Master Sergeant
O-5	Lieutenant Colonel	E-7	Gunnery Sergeant
O-4	Major	E-6	Staff Sergeant
O-3	Captain	E-5	Sergeant
O-2	First Lieutenant	E-4	Corporal
O-1	Second Lieutenant	E-3	Lance Corporal
		E-2	Private First Class
		E-1	Private

Marine Reserves

In addition to active-duty Marines, the Corps maintains a large group of reserves. Reserve personnel undergo the basic Marine training, but instead of serving full-time in the Marines, they serve on a part-time basis while working at other careers. Marine reservists generally meet to train for only one weekend a month plus two weeks in the summer. This system allows reservists to pursue careers outside the military while being paid for continuing their training as Marines. The advantage of the reserve system for the Marine Corps is that

Sergeant Bascom sits on and guards a light armored vehicle while his crew inspects the vehicle and the area. The rank of sergeant is held in high regard in the Marine Corps.

it allows it to maintain a large pool of trained military personnel without having to maintain them full-time. This makes it possible for the Marines to keep their peacetime level at 174,000, yet provides instant, trained additional strength in the event of a war. For example, Marine Corps Reserves were called into action during the Gulf War.

Service in the reserves is the exception to the rule that Marines must be high school graduates. High school seniors can join the reserves and get paid for participating in training one weekend per month. Upon graduation, they then move on to recruit training and skills training.

Careers, Pay, and Benefits

When people think of a career in a military organization such as the Marine Corps, they tend to think in terms of soldiers in combat or in training for combat. Certainly, the philosophy "every Marine a rifleman" and the Corps' pride in its readiness to fight the nation's battles imply opportunities for direct military action. In fact, many Marines serve as members of an infantry division, the primary Marine assault force. Here they take on such jobs as rifleman, machine gunner, mortar man, antitank and assault guided missile man, reconnaissance man, or light armored vehicle (LAV) crewman. Infantry personnel face the brunt of the action when a crisis calls for military force.

Other Marines belong to the combat support units such as the field artillery. The skills they learn

★ 74 ★

in meteorology enable Marines to become field meteorologists, while experience with trajectory and maintaining howitzers qualify Marines for positions such as field artillery batteryman. Armored support units offer positions such as driver, gunner, and loader on a state-of-the-art M-1A1 tank or an assault amphibian vehicle.

Aviation is one of the more glamorous Marine occupations. Highly qualified and trained individuals learn to fly such high-speed, sophisticated aircraft as the Hornet and the Harrier, giant transport planes such as the Hercules, transport helicopters like the Super Stallion and Sea Knight, all-purpose Huey helicopters, and combat helicopters such as the Cobra.

Marines in armored support units learn to operate support vehicles such as this state-of-the-art M-1A1 main battle tank. These Marines are participating in an exercise designed to improve cooperation between U.S. and Croatian military forces.

Special-Duty Careers

Some Marines are specially trained for prestigious guard duty at home, at military bases in foreign countries, on the high seas, and at U.S. government diplomatic outposts scattered around the world. More than 6,600 Marines serve as security guards at naval shore bases. While one of the Marines' primary original functions—that of serving as boarding parties and military police aboard the U.S. Navy ships—became largely obsolete many years ago, approximately six hundred Marines continue to be stationed aboard

 ### Colonel John Glenn, Jr. (1921–)

Born in Cambridge, Ohio, Glenn joined the Marine Corps in 1943 as a fighter pilot. He flew fifty-nine missions during World War II and another ninety missions in Korea. After serving for five years as a test pilot in the 1950s, Glenn was selected as one of the nation's first astronauts. In 1962, he became the first American to orbit the earth in a spaceship. After retiring from the Corps, Glenn entered politics and won election to the U.S. Senate in 1974.

Navy ships. Meanwhile, in recent years the Marines have accepted the honor of potentially hazardous duty as guards at U.S. embassies.

Embassy responsibility grew as a result of modern-day terrorism. For example, in May 1948, a sniper killed U.S. diplomat T.C. Wasson, who was on assignment in Jerusalem. In response, the State Department increased protection at U.S. embassies. In 1949, it called on the Marines to provide security guards for U.S. embassies around the world. Today, these specially trained guards provide protection for embassies in 140 different countries. Equipped only with light arms, the handful of Marines assigned are not expected to defend these embassies against a full-scale attack or riot. Their purpose is to discourage isolated incidents and to hold off danger until local police or armed forces restore order.

Special duty also includes prestigious assignments when a military presence is required for both security and ceremonial reasons. Special-duty Marines serve as honor guards for the president at the White House and the presidential retreat at Camp David as well as at State Department functions.

Many Marines eventually become involved in either attracting new Marines or training recruits. These jobs are so important to the Corps that nearly all enlisted men and women who want a career in the Marine Corps serve part of their time either as a recruiter or as a drill instructor.

Wide Career Opportunities

Many careers in the Marine Corps do not involve direct combat or security. Marines may receive training in more than 180 skills that prepare them for more than three hundred specialized jobs in thirty-four different occupational fields. A few of these occupations are fairly specialized within the military. For example, those who work in ordnance are responsible for inspecting, maintaining, repairing and storing weapons, ammunition, and explosives. Intelligence personnel collect and study information to determine the enemy's strengths and weaknesses. Their sources range from on-site observation to satellite imagery. Avionics is the occupational field that deals with the sophisticated radio and radar equipment needed for a successful and modern aviation force. Careers in this field include aircraft communications/ navigation systems technician, aircraft weapons systems technician, and aircraft electrical systems technician.

The vast majority of Marine Corps occupations involve skills and training that can be applied in civilian life as well as in the military. Enlistment in the Marine Corps can help young people pursuing these careers, not only by providing needed training and experience but also by allowing them to establish a track record. This track record will be useful if they intend to continue their careers after they leave the armed services and join the civilian workforce.

Two Marine Corps drill instructors stand at attention during review on a parade ground. Recruiting and training new Marines is so important that nearly all enlisted men or women who want a career in the Corps serve part of their time as either a recruiter or drill instructor.

Logistics, Supply, and Maintenance

No matter how well trained the Marine or how advanced the equipment, all military operations depend upon being able to get people and equipment *where* they are needed, *when* they are needed. Logistics experts determine the needs of a particular operation and make plans for how the movement of personnel and equipment is to be carried out. Marines trained in supply administration and operations are in charge of

carrying out the logistics by obtaining the necessary supplies and keeping inventories. Marines who work in the logistics and supply field are well trained for such civilian jobs as inventory supervisor, shipping clerk, and freight traffic agent.

Marine mechanics are responsible for ensuring that the equipment is in top working order. While the pilots get most of the attention, they could not perform their jobs without the work of the aircraft

These Marines at the motor transport school are learning to operate a fuel-testing device. Motor transport mechanics are responsible for keeping all motor vehicles and amphibious trucks in working condition.

maintenance crews. The training that Marine aircraft mechanics receive in order to keep expensive and complex military aircraft in working order is equally valuable to commercial aircraft companies. Marine-trained mechanics are much sought after in the civilian sector. Similarly, motor transport personnel, who are responsible for keeping all motor vehicles and amphibious trucks in good operation, can transfer their skills to careers as auto and truck mechanics.

Engineering and Technical Support

Marines rely heavily on engineers and construction workers to provide them with facilities they need both at home and in the field. This includes such diverse needs as aircraft runways, oil storage facilities, and barracks. Jobs available to Marines include combat engineer, bulk fuel specialist, heavy equipment operator, and metalworker. These Marines learn skills in planning construction projects and in operating heavy machinery that are highly sought by civilian construction firms.

Similarly, Marine Corps operations cannot run smoothly without utilities, which may not be sufficiently available in the areas to which they are sent. Marines pursuing a career in the utilities field learn how to install, operate, and maintain such essentials as water supply, plumbing and sewage facilities, electricity, heating, and refrigeration. Many Marines involved in this area pursue civilian careers as electricians, refrigeration mechanics, or plumbers. The

An avionics electronic technician inspects a machine to make sure it is working properly. The Marine Corps depends on technicians to repair and maintain vital equipment.

Marine Corps also relies heavily on electronic equipment in meteorological instruments, photographic equipment, electrical simulators, and navigational controls. Marines who train to become electronics maintenance experts handle these jobs.

Clear communications are essential to any military operation. Wars have been won and lost based on whether vital information was relayed to various units quickly, accurately, and secretly. To aid in this area, the Marine Corps trains personnel in all aspects of radio, satellite, and wire/cable communications. Jobs in this area include wireman, field radio operator, and communication center operator and are easily transferable to commercial fields such as radio, TV, and telephone communications.

Military personnel run the risk of encountering nuclear, biological, or chemical (NBC) contamination in the field. The Marine Corps employs NBC defense specialists trained in the use of nuclear radiation and chemical agent detection

There are many administrative jobs available in the Marine Corps. This disbursing clerk is updating a Marine's military pay record by computer.

instruments. They are also trained in decontamination measures in cases in which radioactive, biological, or chemical weapons have been used by the enemy and in inspection of chemical warfare protection equipment. NBC defense specialists are in demand in civilian laboratories dealing with nuclear, biological, or chemical contamination.

Accurate weather reports are crucial to the Marines, especially in coordinating air support. Weather service personnel are trained to collect, record, and analyze meteorological data to keep decision-makers informed of atmospheric conditions.

Administrative Careers

As with any large organization, the Marine Corps requires administrative experts to maintain an efficient operation. Careers in personnel and administration are available to Marines with a talent for organization. This involves compiling and sorting written and automated records on personnel, equipment, available funds, supplies, bills, and other records.

Auditing, finance, and accounting employees help the Marine Corps keep track of financial records, including paying salaries, disbursing funds allotted from the government, and estimating budget needs for the future. This includes occupations such as auditing technician, travel clerk, and personal financial records clerk. Computers have become essential in such administrative tasks. As a result the Marine Corps also trains and employs experts in data systems and computer programming.

While the Marines place a heavy emphasis on a strict code of values, they are not immune from human nature, and so a law enforcement presence is necessary. The Marine Corps trains its own military police, who enforce laws and military orders and control traffic. They guard not only military prisoners but also prisoners of war.

The Marine Corps also has more than four hundred practicing lawyers in its Judge Advocate Division as well as law clerks, court reporters, and stenotype operators in its Legal Services. Marine lawyers work on such diverse cases as protection of the Marine

Corps trademark, court martials, international law issues such as treaty and arms control agreements, national cases involving issues such as the environment and discrimination, and routine legal matters such as wills and compliance with new laws.

Training and experience in all administrative careers are easily transferable to the civilian world.

Personnel Support Careers

The Marine Corps also offers thousands of jobs in careers that are seldom thought of as military careers but which provide important support for Corps operations. The Corps depends upon draftsmen, architects, and cartographers to make needed mechanical drawings and maps. Lithographers then transfer this information as well as aerial photographs to multicolored maps and also provide informational and psychological warfare materials. The occupational field of training and audiovisual support operates still, motion picture, and aerial cameras, develops and edits film, and provides illustrations for written materials.

Food service specialists take responsibility for planning and preparing meals for the thousands of Corps members. Other Marines are involved in the simple but essential task of transporting Marines and their belongings to various bases around the country and overseas.

Public relations is an important part of the Marine Corps. Because their role is less clearly defined than that of the three larger armed services, the Corps pays

Food service specialists are responsible for planning and preparing meals for thousands of Corps members. This Marine is making cookies for the evening meal at a camp in Korea.

close attention to telling its story to the public and providing resources for media people seeking information. The Marine Corps also trains people in print and broadcast journalism, marketing, public speaking, advertising, and public and community relations.

All occupations in the personnel support field are virtually identical to their counterparts in civilian life.

Music

The Marine Corps is an ideal place for talented young musicians to establish themselves as professionals in their chosen field. Nearly all of the 143 musicians in the Marine Band are career professionals.

The Marine Corps established its own band in 1798 to boost morale and to serve as a goodwill ambassador and as a recruiting aid at public and ceremonial events. Its music has proven so popular that the Marine music program has expanded to include the U.S. Marine Drum and Bugle Corps and twelve Marine Corps Bands in addition to the prestigious U.S. Marine Band. The U.S. Marine Band, called the "president's own,"[1] plays more than two hundred times each year at the White House, while each of the other Marine Corps bands averages over three hundred performances per year in communities throughout the nation.

Prospective musicians are invited to audition for a spot in one of the Marine Corps bands as positions become available. People who audition for the band are not obligated to join the Corps if they fail to qualify for a spot. Those who win acceptance into the top Marine Band are the only Marines who are not required to go through the thirteen-week basic training program. Any

John Philip Sousa (1854–1932)

A native of Washington, D.C., Sousa was only thirteen years old when he enlisted as an apprentice in the U.S. Marine Corps band and seventeen years old when he conducted an orchestra in a Washington theater. In 1880, he was appointed director of the Marine Band. During his twelve years in that position, he established his reputation as the "March King," with such compositions as "The Stars and Stripes Forever," and he led the band to international fame.

The Marine Corps has a highly renowned music division. This Marine sergeant plays her trumpet during a Marine Corps birthday pageant.

musician who qualifies for a spot in any of the bands is guaranteed that assignment through the term of his or her enlistment. Earning a spot in a Marine Corps band entitles the musician to attend the highly respected Armed Forces School of Music to further improve his or her skills.

Pay and Benefits

Pay in the Marine Corps is based on pay grade and duty location. Advances in pay grade are based on performance as well as rank and time served. Every Marine has an equal opportunity to train and advance. As of July 1, 2000, newly enlisted Marines start at $930 per month. At four months of service, or shortly after completion of basic training, the pay increases to $1,005 per month. Top-level enlisted Marines with twenty years of service can earn $3,473.40 per month. Marines earn additional income for serving on sea duty, foreign duty, or special assignments such as aviation. Marine reservists calculate their monthly earnings for weekend training by dividing the normal monthly pay for their grade by thirty and multiplying by four.

Newly commissioned second lieutenants start out at $1,926.30 per month. Senior-level officers with 26 years of experience can earn over $11,000 per month. Marines serving in specialized professional occupations such as judge advocates receive pay comparable to that for similar civilian jobs.

In an effort to attract and keep outstanding young prospects, the Marine Corps offers a host of benefits.

In addition to the generous educational benefits described in chapter three, Marines get free medical and dental care and thirty days of paid leave each year of service. In some cases, a housing allowance is added to their pay. Those who serve a long time in the Marine Corps are entitled to keep their medical and dental benefits after leaving the Corps as well as a generous pension.[2] Most Marines who retire with these benefits are young enough to begin earning additional money in a civilian career.

While in the Corps, Marines (including those serving part-time in the Reserves) are able to take advantage of numerous opportunities, discounts, and other fringe benefits. They are entitled to utilize the Marine Corps' legal services and career counseling, on-base discount supermarkets and department stores, and discounts on air travel. The Special Services section provides Marines on base with activities such as movies, bowling, swimming, golf, camping, and boating. It also lends equipment to Marines wishing to participate in these activities.

Travel is a given in the Marine Corps, where transfers and promotions are frequent. Marines may serve on bases located on both coasts of the United States and in Hawaii and on foreign bases in places such as Japan, the Philippines, the Balkans, and Germany.

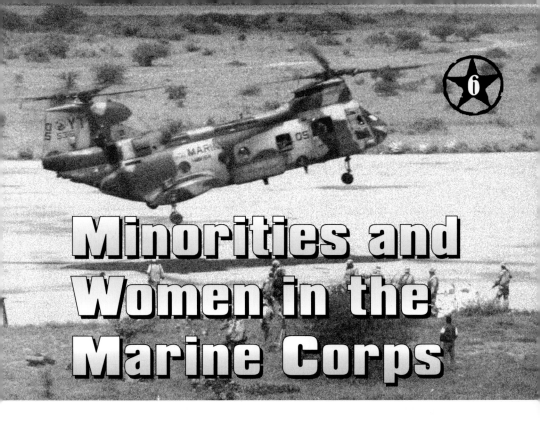

Minorities and Women in the Marine Corps

Although the Marine Corps takes pride in adhering to an unwavering code of conduct, it has evolved along with society. For more than a century, the Marine Corps was all white and all male. This reflected the prevailing opinion of American military leaders that women and members of minority groups, particularly African Americans, were not desirable soldiers.

History of Minorities in the Corps

Free African Americans eagerly joined the American cause early in the Revolutionary War, only to find a lukewarm welcome in most instances. On November 12, 1775, General George Washington signed an official order barring the enlistment of African Americans in the American Army. A series of defeats, however, put Washington's army in a desperate position in which it could not afford to turn down help from anyone. For the remainder of the war, African-American soldiers were scattered among a number of regiments. John Paul Jones, who commanded a number of Marines during his exploits on the high seas, had no qualms about including African Americans in his crew.

Once the war was over, however, Americans resumed their objections to minorities in the military. In the 1798 Act that established the Marine Corps, Congress expressly banned African Americans, American Indians, and those of mixed race from enlisting in the Corps.

During the later years of the Civil War, the U.S. Army accepted hundreds of thousands of African-American soldiers, who trained and fought in segregated (all African-American) units under the command of white officers. Yet the Corps remained for whites only, a policy to which the U.S. Army returned following the war. The Marine Corps refused to employ African Americans even as messengers at their headquarters. This situation remained unchanged until the eve of World War II.

Integration of the Marines

The change began in 1941 when President Franklin Roosevelt ordered the formation of special units for African-American Marines. The Marine Corps, and indeed military leaders in the other services, strongly resisted the order. Secretary of the Navy Frank Knox openly doubted the ability of minorities to fight. General Thomas Holcomb warned "there would be a definite loss of efficiency in the Marine Corps if we have to take Negroes."[1]

When on May 20, 1942, under pressure from Roosevelt, the Department of the Navy ordered the Marine Corps to begin recruiting minorities, it resisted even more strongly than the other services. The first African-American Marine unit was the 51st Defense Battalion. Like all the rest of the African-American service units, it saw no combat during the war. It was assigned to patrol only areas that white Marines had already secured. No African Americans were made officers during the war.

Meanwhile, the Marines participated in an experiment involving Navajo Indians. Frustrated by the enemy's ability to crack their codes, the Marines agreed to use Navajo to send and receive messages along combat lines. The Navajo developed a code with their own language that only other Navajo could decipher. Although most Marines did not know exactly what the Navajo were doing in their units, they accepted them. The flawless performance of the Navajo Code Talkers, as they were called, was a key factor in the Corps' success in storming the Pacific islands.

Despite the Code Talkers' success and Marine Corps General Vandegrift's assessment that "the Negro Marines are no longer on trial; they are Marines," the Corps backslid on integration after the war.[2] By early

The Marine Corps used Navajo Indians to communicate along combat lines during World War II. Known as Code Talkers, they developed a code, using the Navajo language, that only they could decipher.

1947, the only African Americans in the Marine Corps were stewards, whose primary job was to serve food.

On July 26, 1948, President Harry Truman issued Executive Order 9981, which said: "It is hereby declared to be the policy of the President that there shall be equality of treatment and opportunity for all persons in the armed forces."[3] Favored Republican presidential candidate Thomas Dewey opposed racial integration in the armed forces. But upon Truman's upset election later that year, the Marines had no choice but to remove all policies prohibiting integration, which they did on November 18, 1949.

Still the Marine Corps moved slowly. At the start of the Korean War, there were only 1,075 African Americans in the Corps, virtually all of them in service positions. High combat losses, however, forced the Marines to replace white soldiers on the front lines with trained African Americans. Their performance erased all doubts the leadership had about the wisdom of integration. Within two years, the Marine Corps went from the most segregated of the armed services to the least. The number of African-American Marines swelled to 15,000. All units of the Corps were fully integrated, and assignments were based on need and ability rather than race.

Minorities in Today's Marine Corps

The Marine Corps experienced some racial problems within the ranks during the civil rights movement in the late 1960s. These problems hit a peak in 1970, when the Corps reported 1,096 violent racial incidents. Corps leadership, however, moved aggressively to eliminate Marines who had a problem with racial equality. In 1972, General Cushman stated, "Those individuals who cannot or will not abide by this principle should seek other employment. There is no room for such Marines in our Corps today."[4]

The numbers demonstrate the progress the Marine Corps has made. From 1973 to 1981, the proportion of African Americans in the Corps rose from 13.7 percent to 22 percent. The proportion of African-American officers went from 1.5 percent to 4 percent. In 1984, the Marine Corps decorated its first two African-American generals.

Today, about 20,000 of the 174,000 Marines are African-American. The Marine Corps still cannot match the Army's record in finding and promoting African-American officers; Marine officer ranks remain around 6 percent African-American. However, opportunity for minorities wishing to advance in the Marine Corps is not lacking. According to military author

Marine Sergeant C. Banks, Jr., gives food to a young Haitian boy. The Marines participated in local relief efforts by transporting and delivering food to the inner city of Cap Haitien, Haiti.

Thomas Ricks, "Race simply doesn't appear to be an issue. As career Marines, [they] have far more in common with one another than they do with members of their races outside the military."[5] The Corps' promotional materials make a point of featuring minority Marines prominently.

History of Women in the Corps

Before the twentieth century, few Americans could even conceive of the idea of women serving in the armed forces in any capacity other than as nurses. During the First World War, however, people recognized that there were many tasks in the operation of the modern military that had nothing to do with combat and that could be handled by women as well as men. The Marine Corps was one of the first armed services to take on women as reserves for such administrative jobs as clerks, secretaries, and receptionists during World War I. This freed more male Marines to take part in combat.

With the end of the war, however, the manpower shortage ended and men resumed all jobs. The Marine Corps did not employ women again until World War II. This time the demands for expanded Marine Corps military operations in the Pacific led to a large influx of women. Around 20,000 women joined the Marine Reserves and took over positions in communications and supply. They served as mechanics, drivers, and air traffic controllers in addition to administrative office duties.

During World War I, the Marine Corps took women on as Reserves to perform administrative jobs, freeing more men for combat. Shown is the famous actress Lillian Russell in her Marine Corps Woman Reserve uniform.

In 1948, in recognition of the value of the more than 300,000 women who served in the armed forces during World War II, Congress passed the Women's Armed Services Integration Act. This allowed women to become regular members of the Marine Corps and not just wartime Reserves.

A major effort to recruit women into the armed services during the Korean War yielded poor results, convincing military planners that women would never play a significant role in the American military. Their expectations appeared to be confirmed over the next twenty years as the numbers of women joining the armed services dwindled to barely 20,000 at the height of the Vietnam War in 1967.

In the 1970s, the situation changed due to the shift to an all-volunteer military and the influence of the feminist movement. The number of female enlistees in the military almost doubled between 1977 and 1980.

Women in Today's Marine Corps

The United States today relies more heavily on women to staff its military than any other major country in the world. Nearly 200,000 women serve in today's armed forces, roughly 14 percent of the total.

The Marine Corps continues to have a lower percentage of women than other armed services. This is partly because the Corps has been outspokenly proud of its toughness and has promoted itself as a fortress of masculine values, and partly because the Marine Corps has a higher percentage of personnel in combat units, from which women are still prohibited. Currently the Corps has about seven thousand enlisted women and six hundred female officers. According to Thomas Ricks, the Marine Corps also fares slightly worse than other armed services in polls that ask

Although women are not allowed in combat units in the Marine Corps, there are opportunities in combat aircraft positions. Captain Sarah Deal was the first female Marine Corps helicopter pilot.

military personnel if they have been sexually harassed. On the other hand, he notes that some of the differences may come from the fact that the Marine Corps is more tolerant of criticism than the other services and so its personnel may feel more free to express their views.

Still, the role of women in the Marine Corps has expanded over the years. Since 1987, women have been allowed to participate in weapons training, and they are held to the same standards as males on the rifle range. Currently, women Marines receive basic recruit training at the same facilities as men, where they have the same curriculum, although they train in separate battalions.

Though banned from combat occupations in the infantry, armor, and special operations units, women have moved into combat aircraft, surface ships, combat-supporting ground units, and positions as embassy guards. During the Gulf War, four Marine women earned the Combat Action Ribbon, an award given to those who have been attacked and returned fire.

Marine barracks are now integrated. The Corps makes a concerted effort to attract and keep qualified female recruits and has expanded its benefits to cover such things as child care. Marine recruiting materials are filled with photographs of female Marines, and the message is clearly intended to appeal to women. One recruiting brochure says, "We don't expect or want you to compromise your femininity. Be a woman. Live the life you want to live."[6]

The Future of the Marine Corps

Unlike the other armed services, the very existence of the Marine Corps has been seriously threatened from time to time. Several presidents, including Andrew Jackson, Theodore Roosevelt, and Harry Truman, have attempted to disband the Corps and assign its duties to Army and Navy units.

The Cold War between the United States and the Soviet Union, which lasted from the late 1940s until 1990, again called into question the purpose of the Marine Corps. There seemed to be no role for the Marine Corps in the stalemate between the huge forces of the Soviet Union and the United States and its allies. The countries prepared for a massive ground war in Europe that had no call for the mobile, lightly armed tactics of the Marines. Furthermore, advances in weapons technology made the success of amphibious assaults more and more doubtful. Indeed, the Marines had not carried out a sea raid in nearly half a century. During the prolonged, stationary war in Vietnam, the Corps basically took on a function that was better suited to the Army.

In view of these facts, Congress in 1966 directed the Commission on Naval Affairs to consider whether the Marine Corps should be abolished or transferred to the U.S. Army. In 1975 the Senate Armed Services Committee ordered yet another examination of the need for the Marine Corps.

In every case the Corps survived, thanks to the intense lobbying of Marines, former Marines, and their supporters. But the Corps is well aware that, in the words of one officer, "the United States does not need a Marine Corps, the United States wants a Marine Corps."[1] Marines have worked tirelessly to adapt themselves to the evolving state of military conflict throughout the years to provide a level of service that the other branches of the military would have a difficult time matching.

In the Corps' favor is the fact that Marines rely less on equipment than do the other military services. This means that they are less vulnerable targets for cuts in times of budget crunches. Even more favorable to the Marines' future is the end of the Cold War, which has brought about a change in U.S. military strategies. The military operations in the past decade have been primarily the kind of low-intensity conflicts with unclear objectives for which the Marines were created. While the Army chafed at going into places such as Somalia and Haiti with no military objectives other than a vague goal of keeping the peace, the Marines welcomed the assignments. Their long tradition of intervention in such volatile situations enabled them to perform brilliantly.

Today's Marines are capable of deploying quickly to any location in the world and sustaining themselves

In an effort to reduce the violence in the city of Mogadishu, the capital of Somalia, the U.S. Marines step up their patrols and arrange to exchange food for weapons. Marines have a long tradition of successful intervention in dangerous situations.

for thirty days without any help. This kind of flexible, fast-strike capability, along with their long tradition of excellence and the cultivation of intense loyalty among Marines past and present, guarantees that the Marines will be an elite and valued fighting force for years to come.

Weapons and Equipment

M-16 Assault Rifle

The most important weapon for any Marine is the rifle. Every Marine must learn to shoot and care for this weapon. Marine recruits are required to memorize a statement that includes the words, "My rifle is my best friend. It is my life. I must master it as I master my life."[1] The M-16 assault rifle is standard issue for Marines. First used in Vietnam, the gas-operated rifle weighs less than eight pounds. It can be fired in both automatic and semiautomatic modes and can deliver 150 rounds a minute.

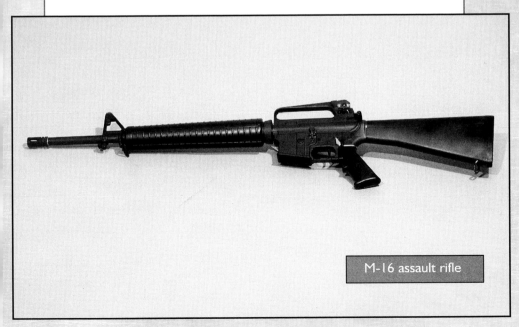

M-16 assault rifle

Corsair F4U

The Corsair was a fighter plane rushed into service for use against the formidable Japanese Zeros during World War II. It featured six wing guns, a maximum speed of 392 miles per hour, and a range of 1,070 miles. The new Corsairs were so desperately needed that the Marines could afford to give their pilots only 20 hours of experience with the new planes before sending them into battle at Guadalcanal, where they quickly established air superiority.

Corsair F4U aircraft

Harrier AV-8

The Harrier is a revolutionary aircraft that combines the best features of an airplane and a helicopter. It can take off vertically, hover in the air, and turn in any direction like a helicopter, yet can fly at near the speed of sound with a maximum range of 2,100 miles. Designed exclusively for the Marine Corps, the Harrier is equipped with bombs and rockets to provide close air support of ground troops. During the Gulf War in 1991, Harriers flew 3,359 sorties. Unfortunately, mechanical problems with the Harrier have resulted in a number of fatal crashes. It is currently being evaluated for safety concerns.

AV-8B Harrier II aircraft

A-6 Intruder

In the 1950s, the British observed that high-altitude bombers were easily spotted by radar and could be destroyed by surface-to-air missiles. This led to the development of fast bombers that could swoop in below radar level to deliver their bombs. The U.S. version of this bomber was the A-6 Intruder. With a range of 1,080 miles and a top speed of 648 miles per hour, the Intruder could be launched from a great distance and could elude most enemy fire. Manned by a crew of two, the Intruder played a major role in Vietnam.

A-6 Intruder aircraft

UH-1 Iroquois

The Bell UH-1 helicopter was originally designated HU-1, from which it got its common nickname, "Huey." Introduced in 1962, the single-rotor, turbine-powered aircraft became the Marine Corps workhorse of the Vietnam War. Its lack of armor or heavy weapons for self-defense left it vulnerable to enemy ground fire. However, with a range of 280 miles and a speed of 135 miles per hour, it served effectively for small troop transport and for evacuating wounded soldiers quickly from the field of battle.

UH-1 Iroquois helicopter ("Huey")

Landing Craft Vehicle, Personnel (LCVP)

During the 1930s, the Corps experimented with modified fishing boats in an effort to develop a boat that could carry fighting men to the beaches and quickly unload them. Working with a design by Andrew Higgins, they added a retractable bow ramp patterned after a Japanese innovation. On August 7, 1942, more than 11,000 Marines landed on Guadalcanal in the new LCVP with a retractable bow ramp. This landing craft would carry Marines to shore for the next 30 years.

Landing Vehicle, Tracked (LVT)

In 1937, the Marines discovered that inventor Donald Roebling had designed a tractor that could travel on both water and land for rescue missions in Florida's swamps. By adding more horsepower, the Marines were able to create a tracked vehicle (one that uses a continuous tread to provide mobility) that could drive through water and over reefs. The machines were ready for use in 1941 and helped make possible the Marine Corps conquest of Pacific islands held by the Japanese during World War II.

Like the LVT, the modern AAV7A1 tracked personnel vehicle is an amphibious vehicle used for carrying troops across water and onto land. The AAV7A1 can carry 25 troops for 300 miles with a top speed of more than 45 miles per hour.

MK-154 Mine Clearance Launcher

The MK-154 mine clearance launcher was developed for use from amphibious vehicles during assault landings. Its purpose is to create a path through a minefield so that Marines can land safely. The MK-154 uses three demolition charges of explosive nylon rope, each of which clears an area 16 meters wide and 100 meters long. Detection devices are then used in the cleared path to make sure that all of the mines have been cleared.

The U.S. military has been using linear demolition charges since the 1960s. During the Vietnam War, the

AAV741 tracked personnel vehicle

demolition charges were towed behind tracked vehicles. While this was useful during ground operations, it did nothing for amphibious operations. The MK-154 mine clearance launcher was developed to meet this need.

Night Goggles

Night goggles are nearly standard issue for Marine Corps combat troops. They gather light through a lens that converts it into electrons. These are passed through a phosphorus plate where the light is multiplied as much as 30,000 times. This makes it possible for the user to see even on a moonless night with cloud cover. Such equipment gives the Marines the capability to fight twenty-four hours a day under any conditions.

"Smart" Bombs

Explosives capable of zeroing in on a specific target are known as "smart" bombs. They have been used since late in the Vietnam War. The first such explosives were controlled by a small television camera placed in the nose of the bomb. The camera was pointed and locked on to a target to which it would guide the bomb. Laser technology has provided an even more sophisticated smart bomb. A low-power laser beam is centered on the target. Specially equipped bombs then home in on the beam. The advantage of the laser system is that more than one aircraft at a time can fire at the target.

Night goggles

CH-53E Super Stallion

Sikorsky Aircraft designed this oversized helicopter especially for the Marine Corps in the 1970s. It featured three engines that provided enough power to carry more than 50 Marines plus equipment to remote locations at a rate of 175 miles per hour. The airplane counterpart to the Super Stallion is the Hercules KC-130, a monster transport plane that can carry 92 fully equipped Marines or 30,000 pounds of cargo.

CH-53E Super Stallion

Chapter Notes

Chapter 1. The Mission and Role of Today's Marines

1. Bruce B. Auster, "One Amazing Kid," *U.S. News & World Report*, June 19, 1995, p. 40.

2. Bernard Halsband Cohen, *The Proud: Inside the Marine Corps* (New York: William Morrow, 1992), p. 83.

3. "Why the Marines?" U.S. Marine Corps brochure, n.d.

Chapter 2. History of the United States Marine Corps

1. Bernard Halsband Cohen, *The Proud: Inside the Marine Corps* (New York: William Morrow, 1992), p. 51.

2. Allan R. Millet, *Semper Fidelis: The History of the United States Marine Corps* (New York: Macmillan, 1980), p. 20.

3. Cohen, p. 54.

4. Linda D. Korazyn, "Marines' First Crucible: Belleau Wood," *American Forces Press Service Page*, n.d., <www.dtic.mil/afps/news/9806183.htm> (June 8, 2001).

5. Victor Krulak, *First to Fight* (Annapolis, Md.: Naval Institute Press, 1984).

6. Cohen, p. 63.

7. Ibid.

8. Ibid., p. 22.

9. Ibid., p. 136.

10. Ibid., p. 93.

11. Ibid., p. 22.

Chapter 3. Recruitment and Training

1. Thomas E. Ricks, *Making the Corps* (New York: Scribner, 1997), p. 19.

2. Ibid., p. 48

3. Marine Corps recruiting poster, n.d.

4. Don Knight, personal communication, January 1, 2001.

Chapter 4. Structure of the Marine Corps

1. "Frequently Asked Questions: Marine Corps End Strengths," *United States Marine Corps History and Museums Division Page*, n.d., <http://64.77.44.2/I_FAQ/09_FAQ.htm> (April 23, 2001).

2. Adapted from John Whiteclay Chambers, *Oxford Companion to American Military History* (Oxford, England: Oxford University Press, 1999), pp. 851 and 853.

Chapter 5 Careers, Pay, and Benefits

1. "USMC Believe It or Not," *Marine Corps League Page*, n.d., <http://www.cris.com/~marine1/usmcbion.htm> (April 23, 2001).

2. "Benefits," *United States Marine Corps Recruiting Page*, n.d., <www.marines.com> (July 3, 2001).

Chapter 6. Minorities and Women in the Marine Corps

1. Michael Lee Lanning, *The African-American Soldier* (Secaucus, New Jersey: Birch Lane Press, 1997), p. 211.

2. Ibid., pp. 212–213.

3. Ibid., p. 221.

4. Ibid., p. 227.

5. Thomas E. Ricks, *Making the Corps* (New York: Scribner, 1997), p. 22.

6. "Where Is That Girl . . .," U.S. Marine Corps brochure, n.d.

Chapter 7. The Future of the Marine Corps

1. Thomas E. Ricks, *Making the Corps* (New York: Scribner, 1997), p. 191.

Weapons and Technology

1. "United States Marine Corps Rifleman's Creed," *Marine Corps League Page*, n.d., <http://www.pos.net/Marine/rifle/htm > (May 31, 2001).

Glossary

amphibious warfare—Method of fighting in which ground forces are transported and attack from the sea.

audit—A review of records to make sure they are accurate.

avionics—The technology of piloted aircraft.

corps—A group of persons, especially trained military personnel, who work together to accomplish their responsibilities.

deploy—Move into position.

elite—Special, exceptional, established as better than the ordinary.

evacuation—Removal; in the military it especially refers to removing wounded and endangered troops from combat zones.

guerrillas—Military fighters who employ hit-and-run tactics, usually against a more powerful enemy.

guidance systems—Technology that directs missiles to their targets.

Leathernecks—Nickname for the Marines taken from the leather collars they wore as part of their uniforms in the early nineteenth century.

logistics—the science of getting people and supplies to where they are needed in an orderly and efficient manner.

meteorology—The science that deals with the atmosphere, especially the weather.

militia—A group of nonprofessional soldiers organized for military service.

mobile defense—A strategy of repelling an attack that relies on swift movements and flexibility rather than staying in one position and awaiting the attack.

no-fly zone—An area in which military flight is prohibited.

ordnance—Military supplies such as weapons and ammunition.

perimeter—The outside border of an area.

retractable—Able to put into use or to remove out of the way, as the situation requires.

seaborne raids—Sudden attacks along a coast carried out by soldiers carried in ships.

stalemate—Situation in which neither of two adversaries can gain an advantage over the other.

stationary war—Military action in which the armies stay in one place to defend a particular area.

surface-to-air missile—Also known as a SAM; an explosive launched from the ground against aircraft.

trajectory—The arc that a thrown or launched object travels before it hits the ground.

warrior training—A system of Marine Corps instruction that teaches the basic elements of combat and prepares recruits mentally to handle the stress of combat.

Further Reading

Aaseng, Nathan. *Navajo Code Talkers*. New York: Walker and Co., 1992.

Green, Michael. *The United States Marine Corps*. Mankato, Minn.: Capstone Press, 1998.

Halasz, Robert. *The U.S. Marines*. Brookfield, Conn.: Millbrook Press, 1993.

Rowan, N.R. *Women in the Marines: The Boot Camp Challenge*. Minneapolis: Lerner Publishing, 1993.

Rummel, Jack. *The U.S. Marine Corps*. Broomall, Pa.: Chelsea House, 1990.

Warner, J.F. *The U.S. Marine Corps*. Minneapolis: Lerner Publishing, 1991.

Internet Addresses

United States Marine Corps Page
<http://www.usmc.mil>

Marine Corps League Page
<http://www.mcleague.org>

United States Marine Corps Recruiting Page
<http://www.marines.com>

Index